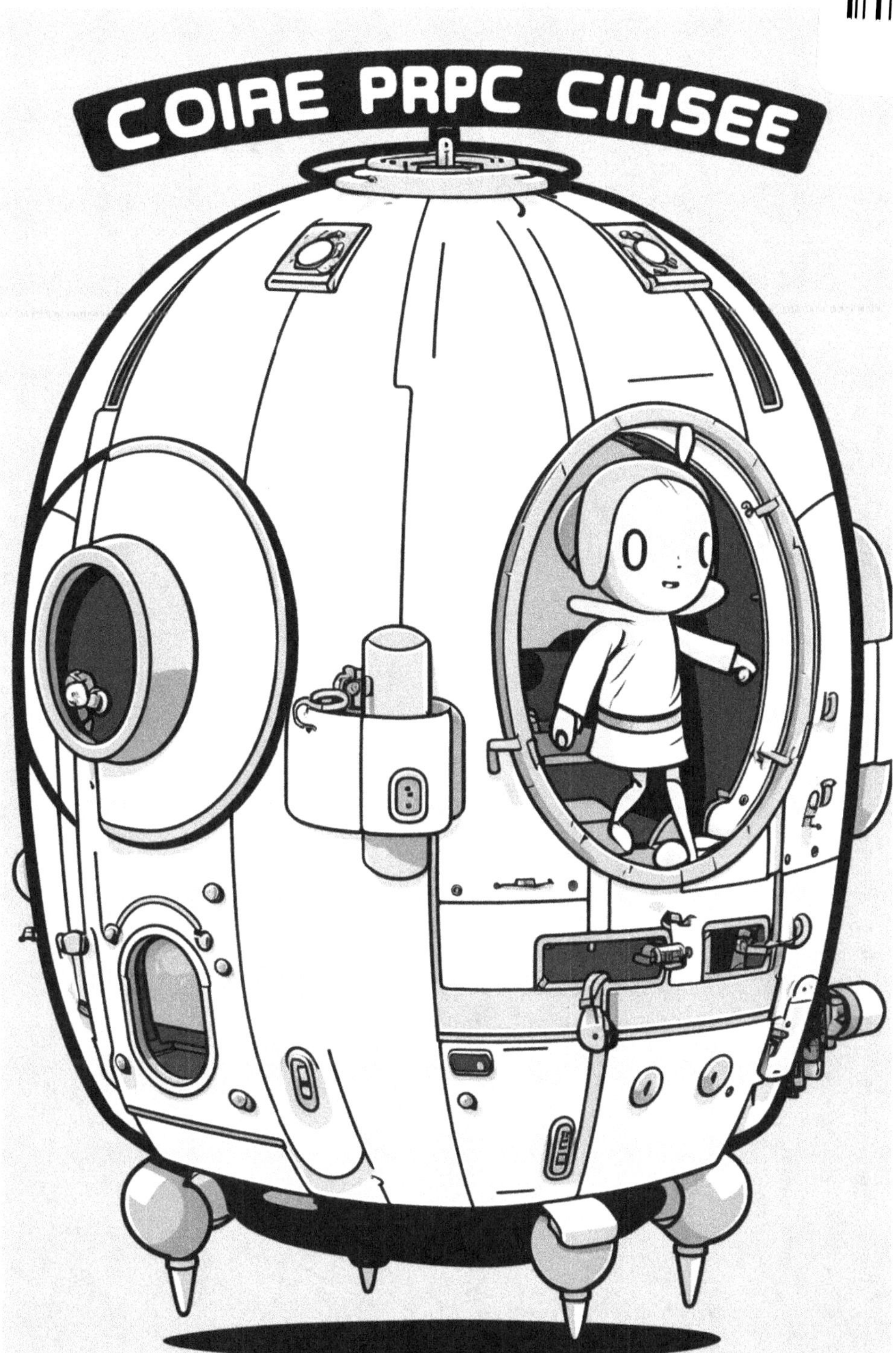

THIS COLORING BOOK
BELONGS TO:

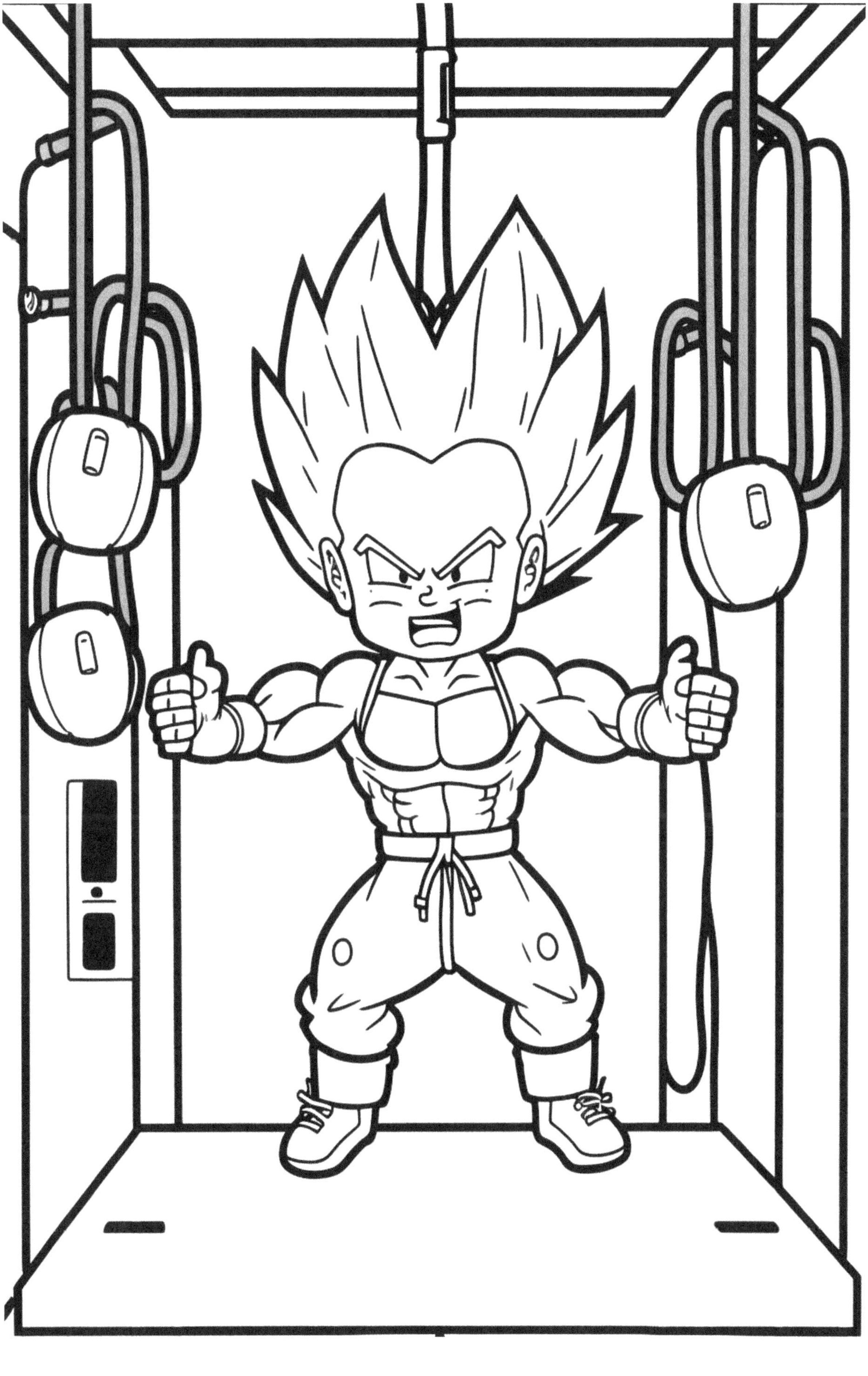

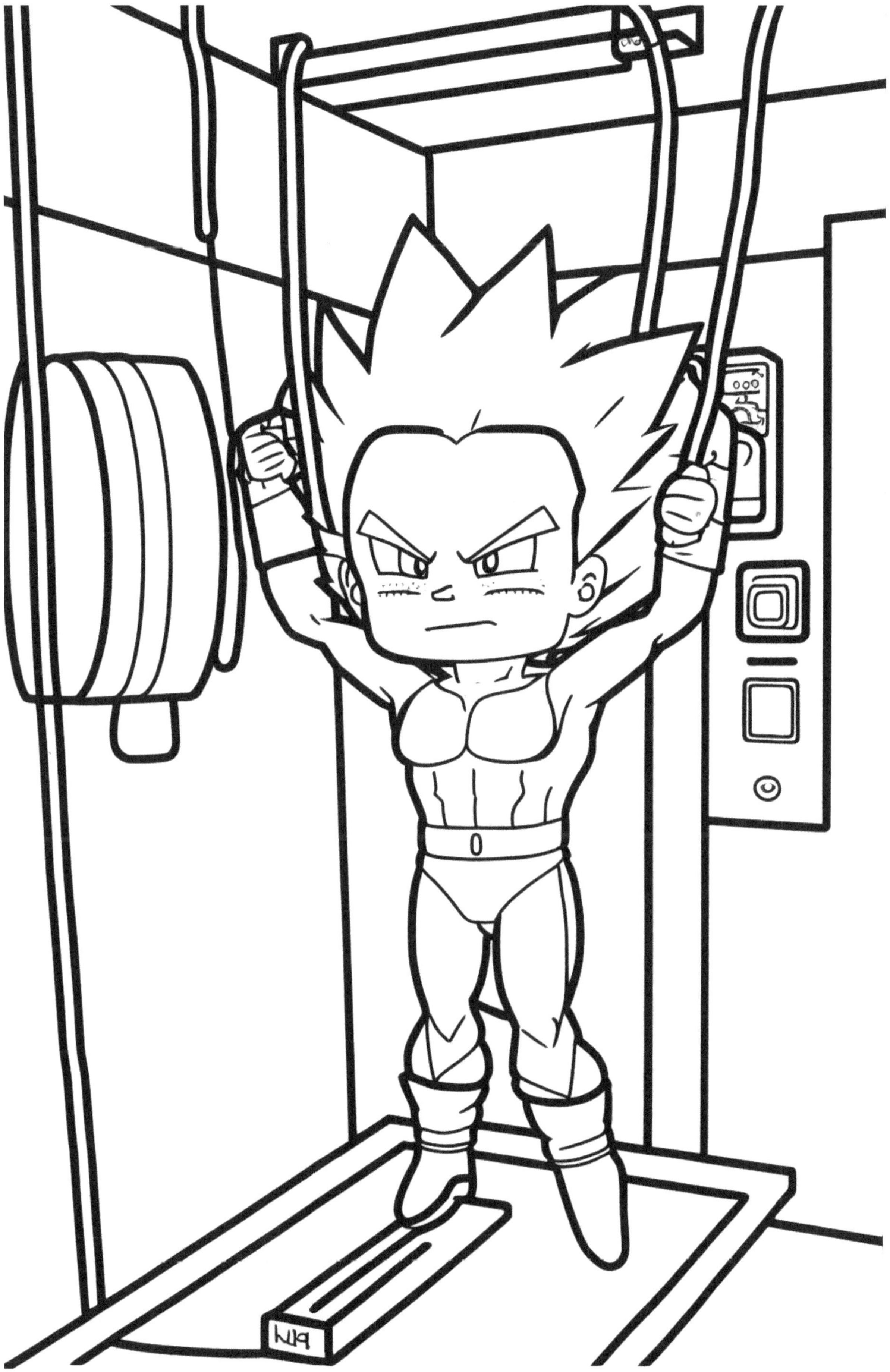

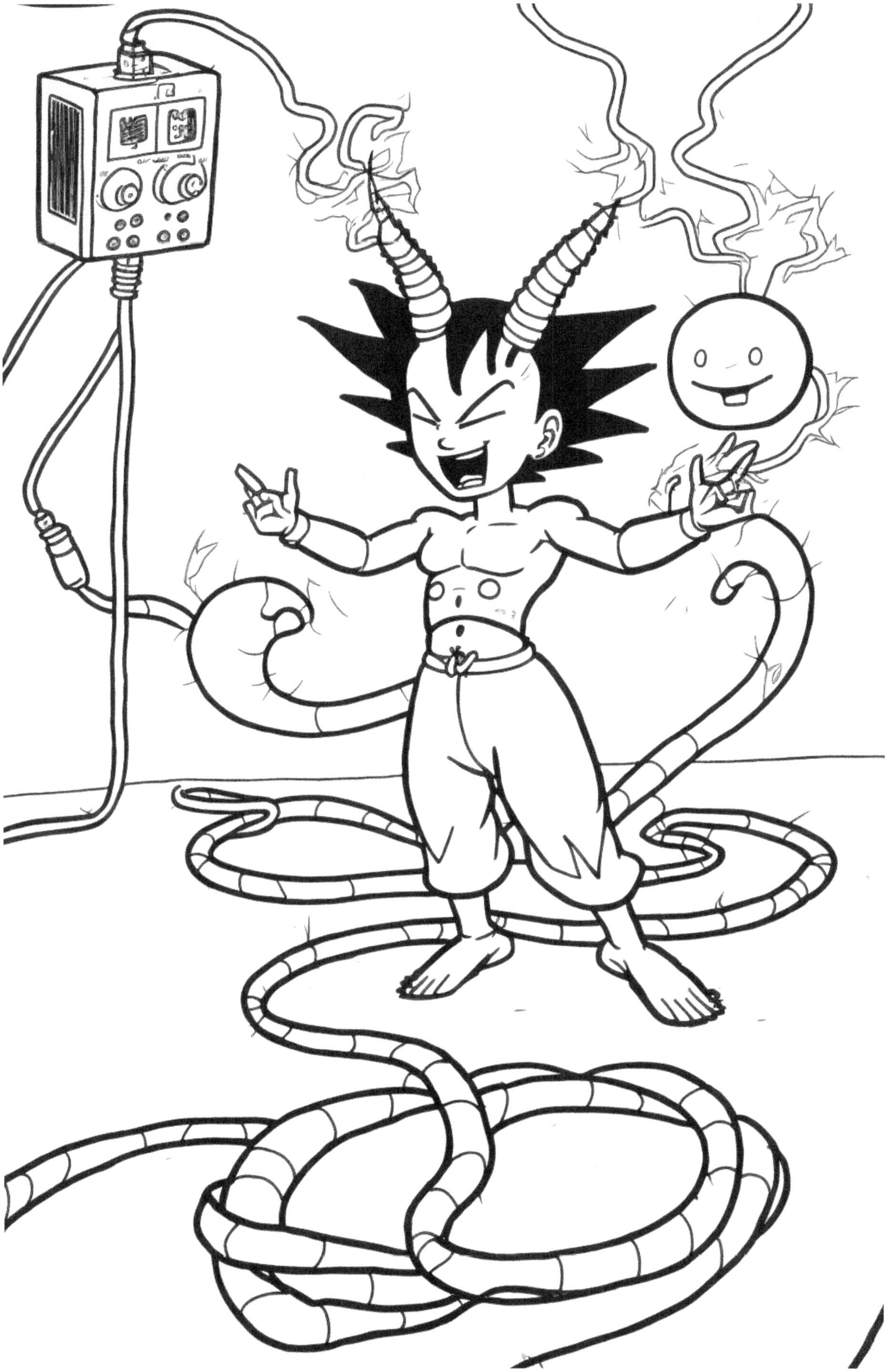

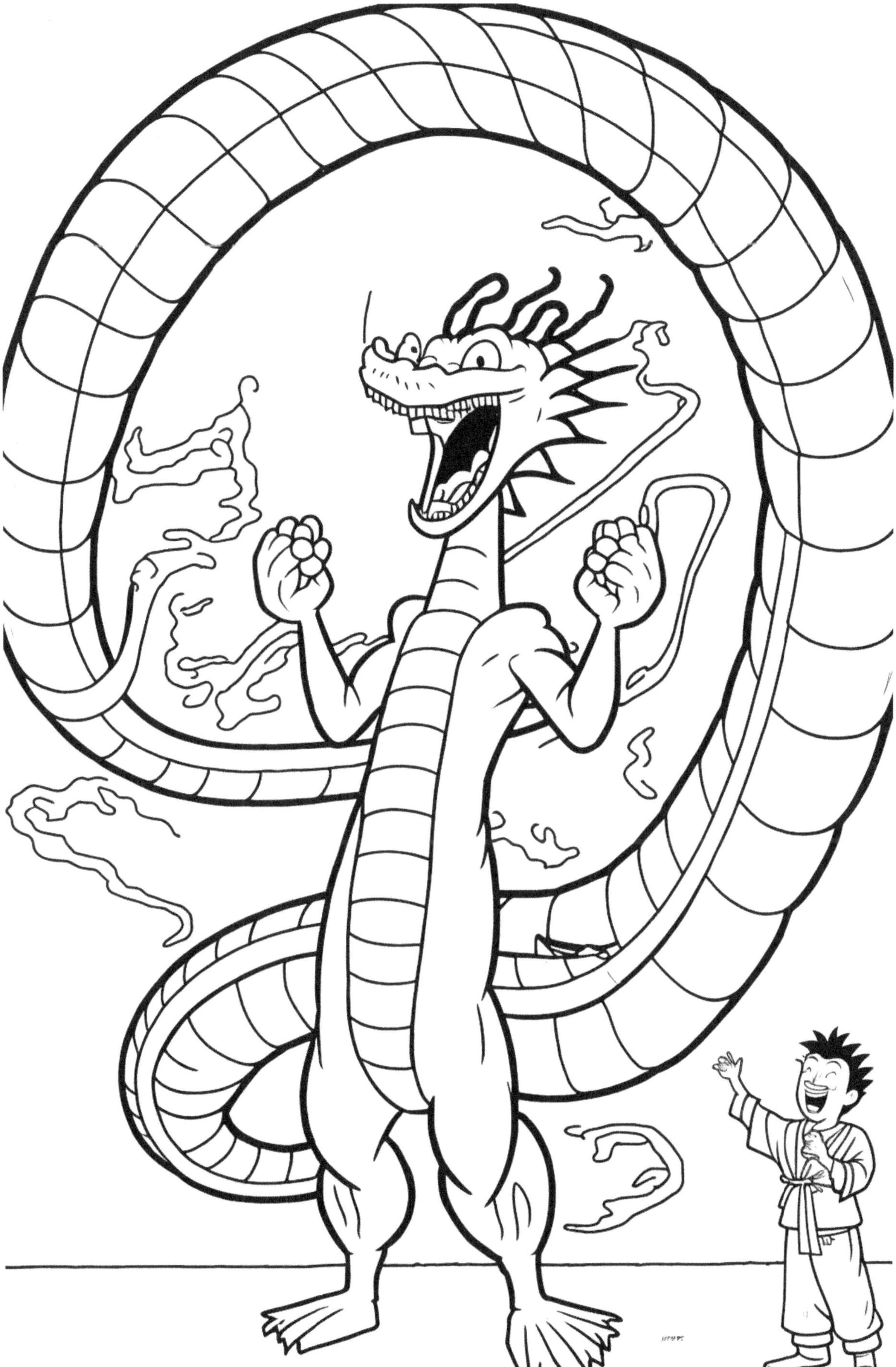

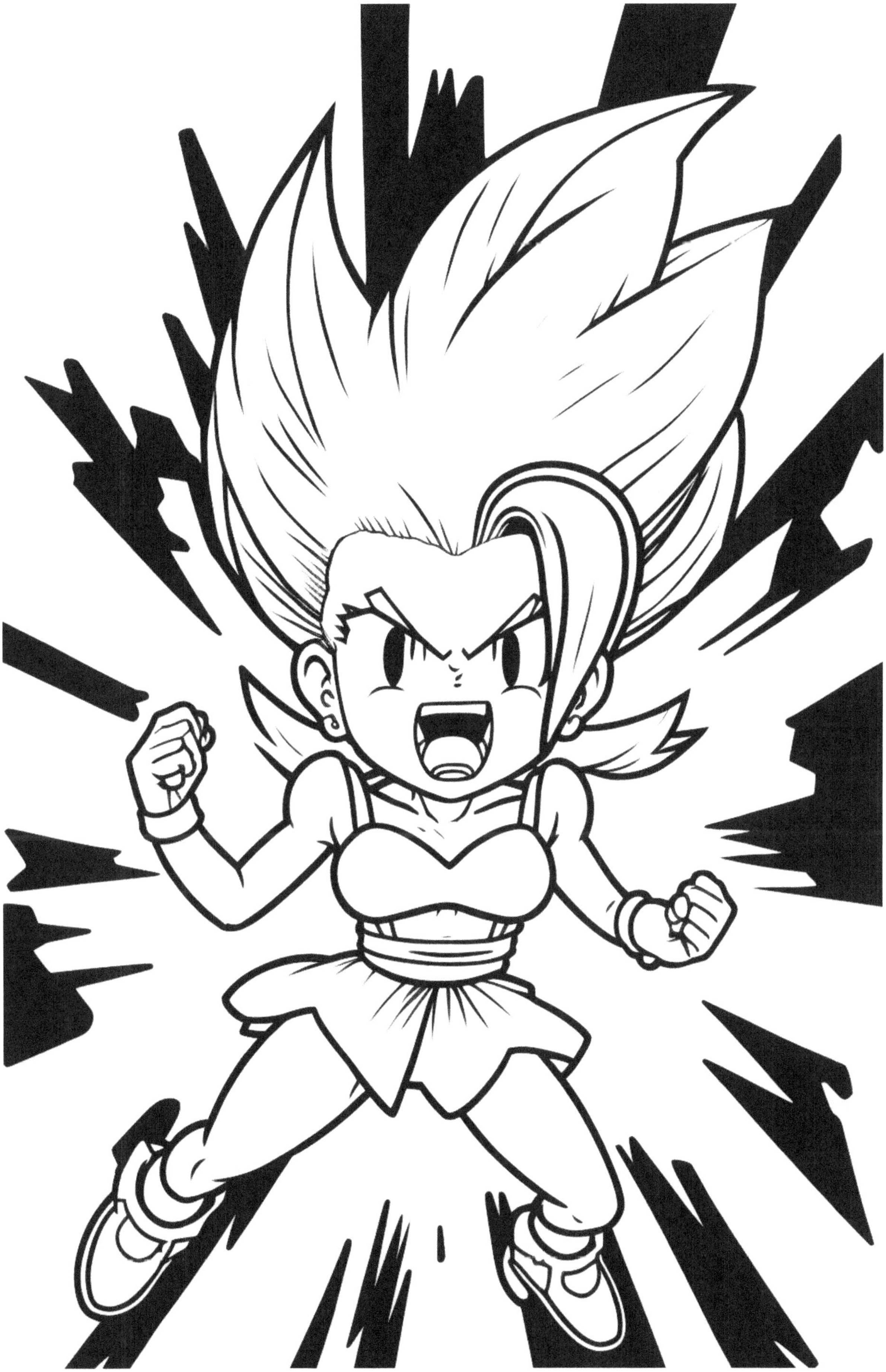

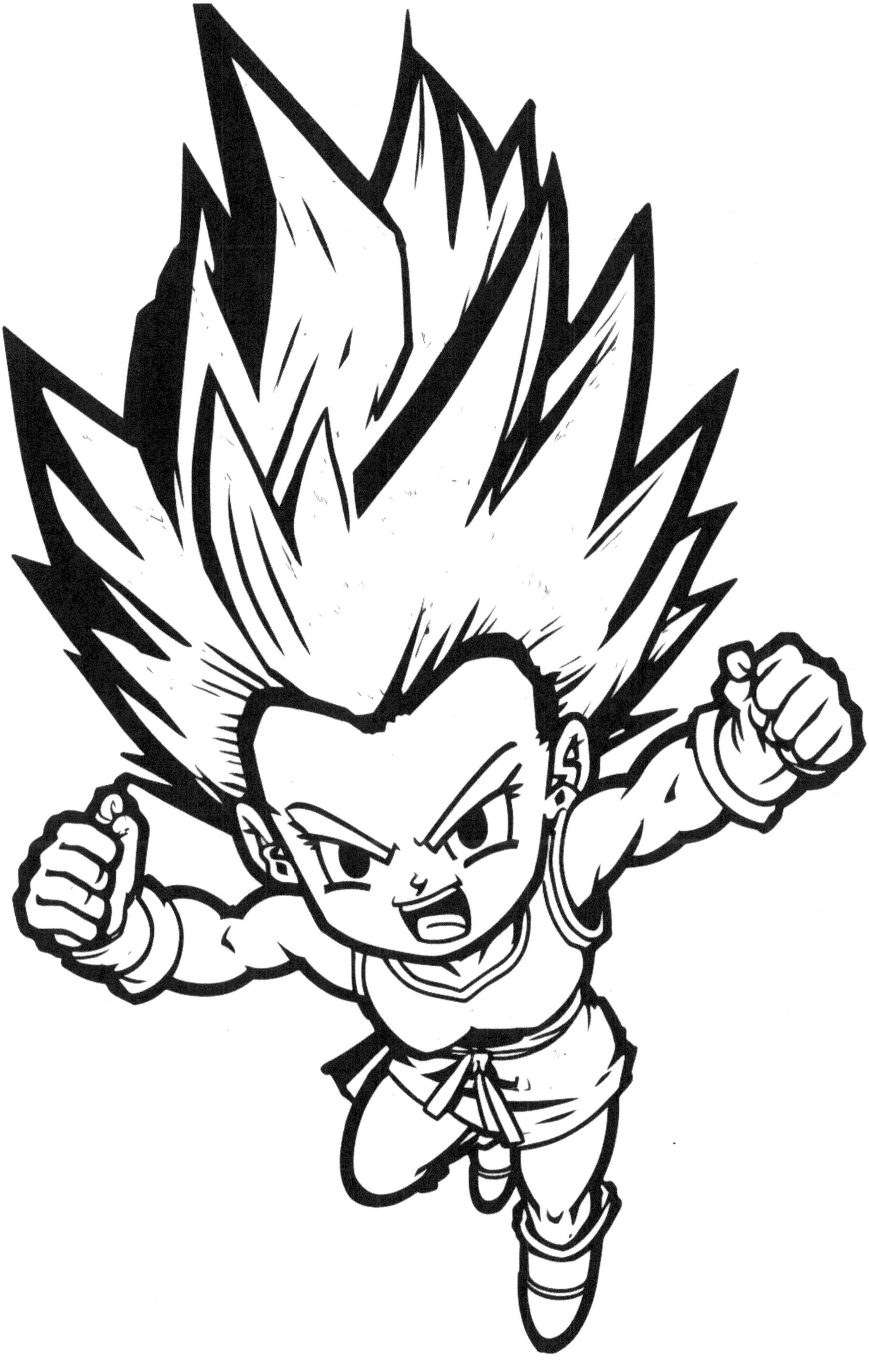

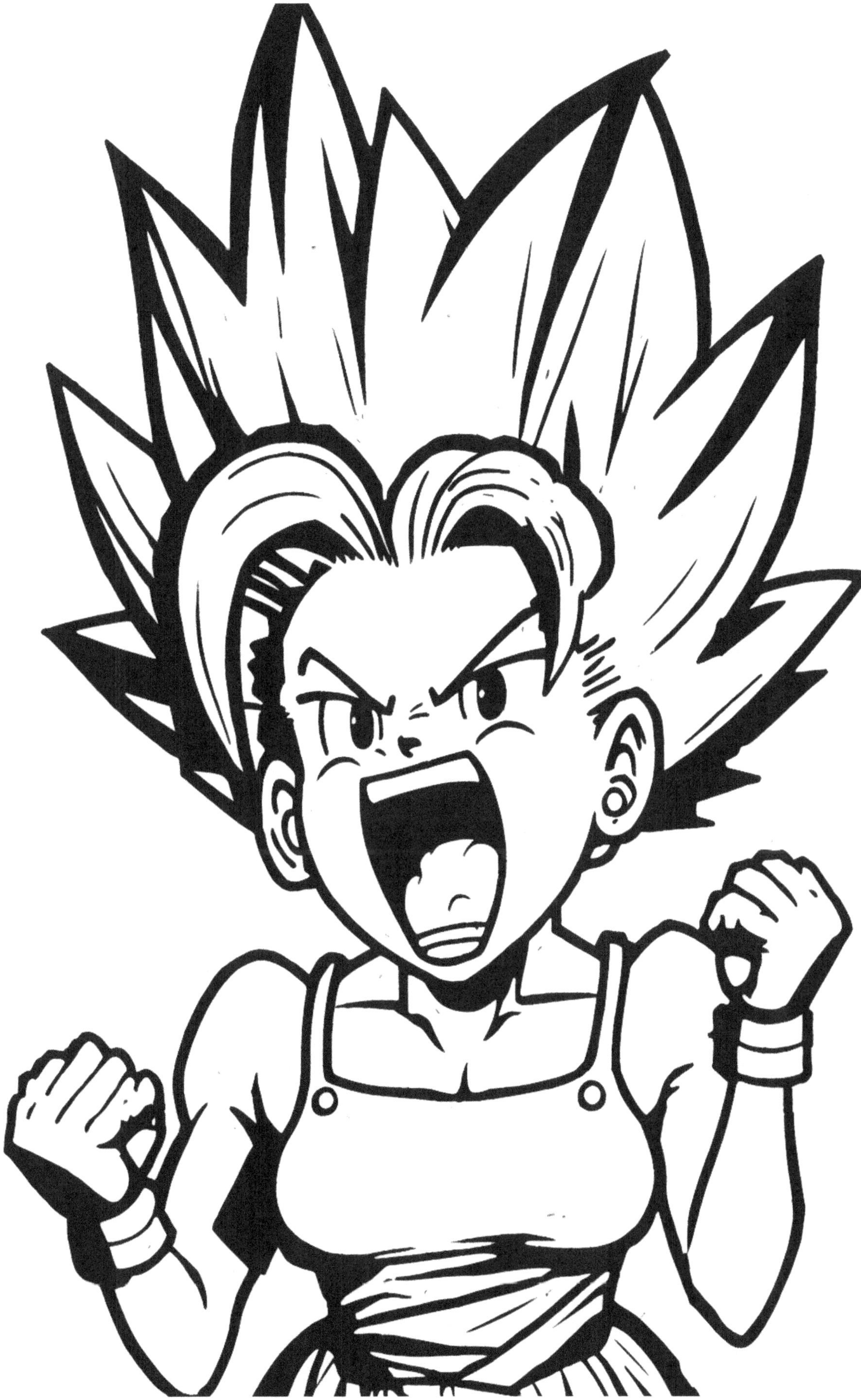

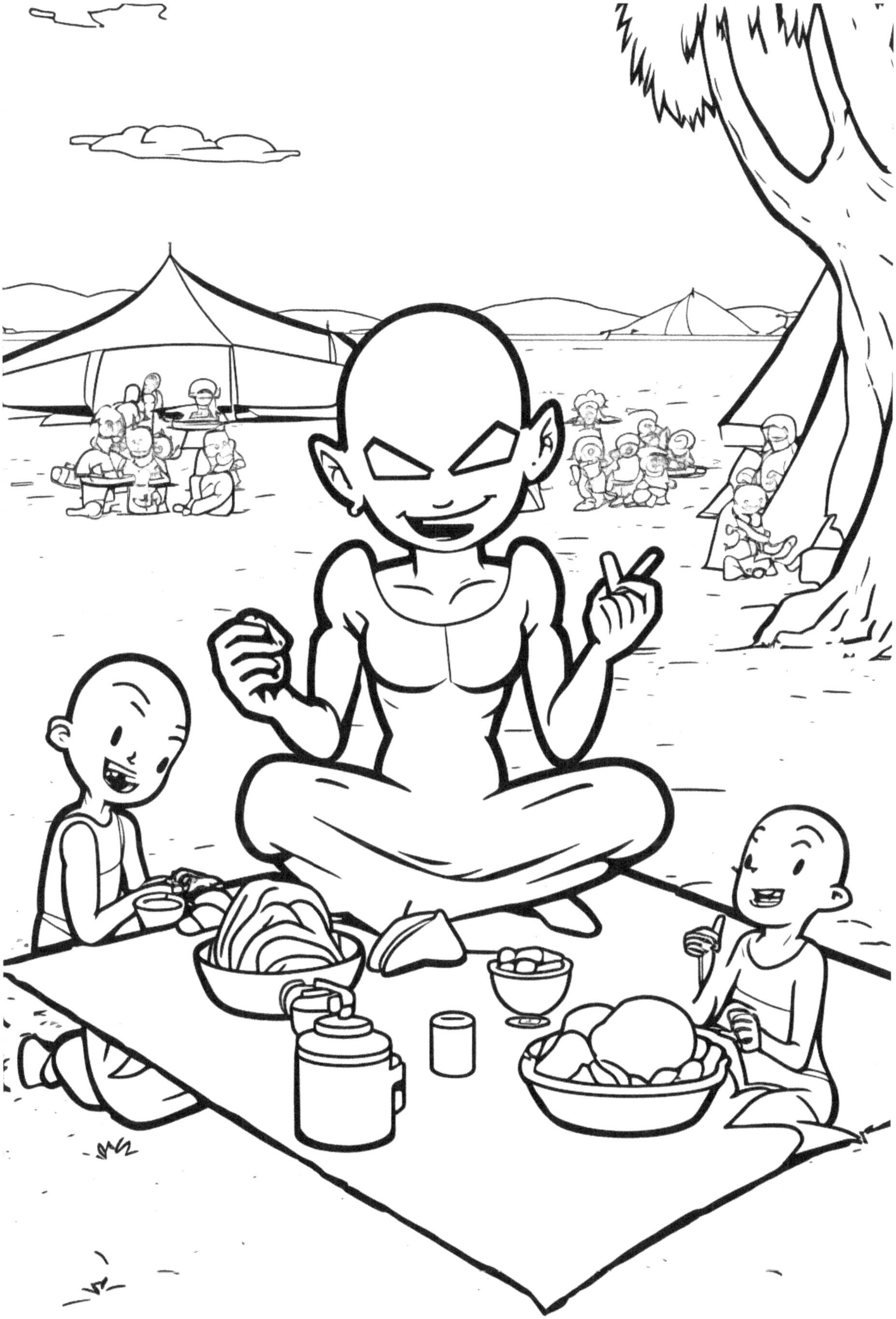

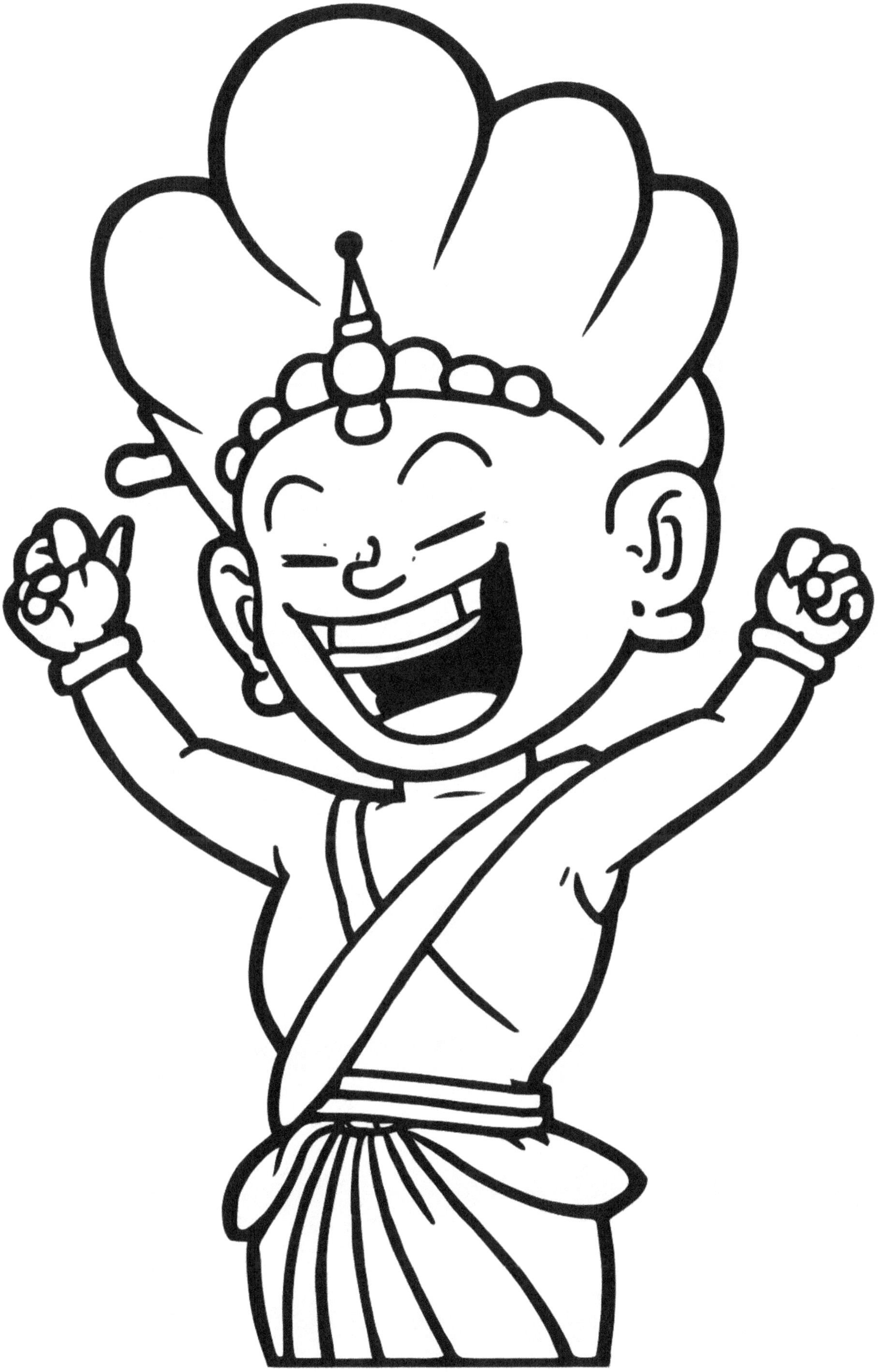

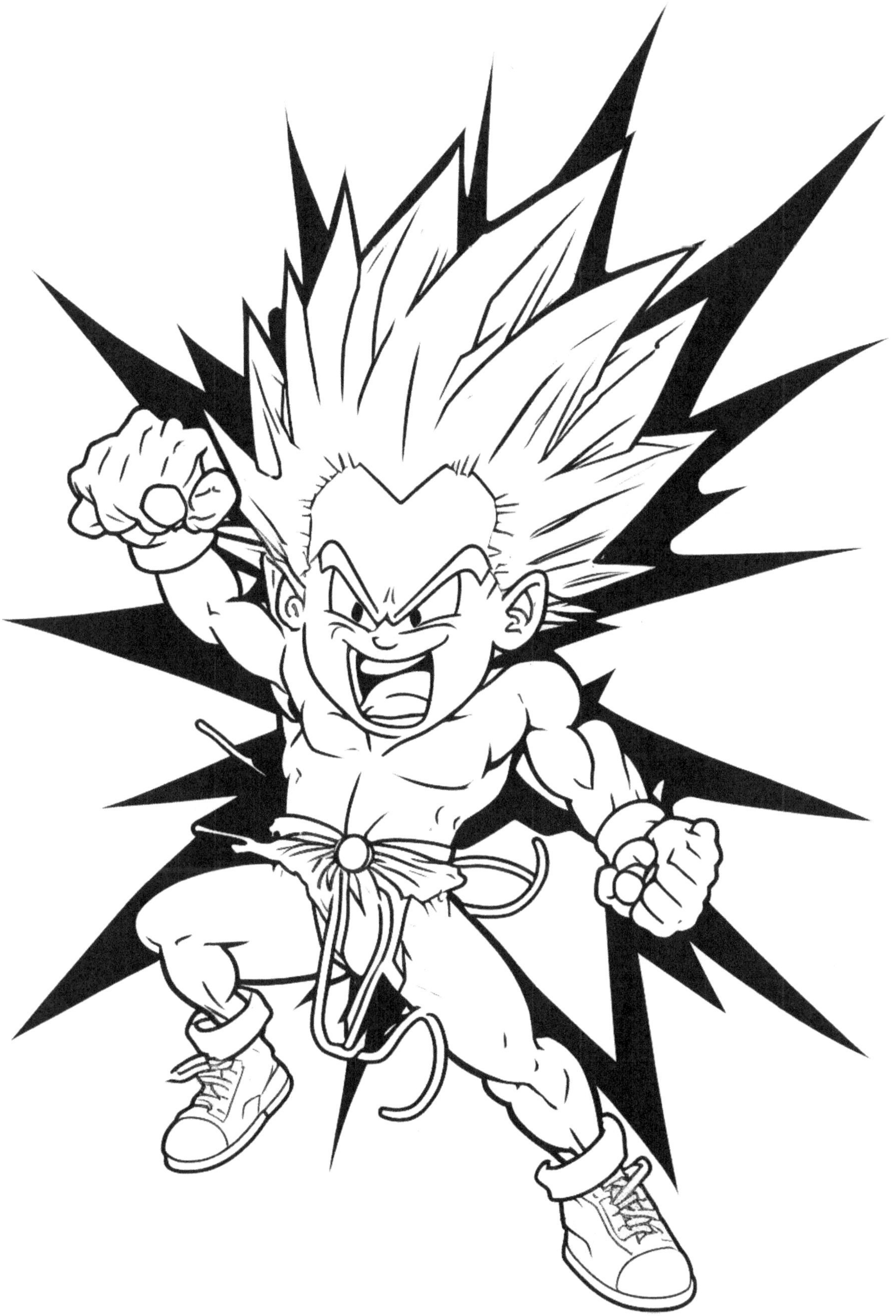

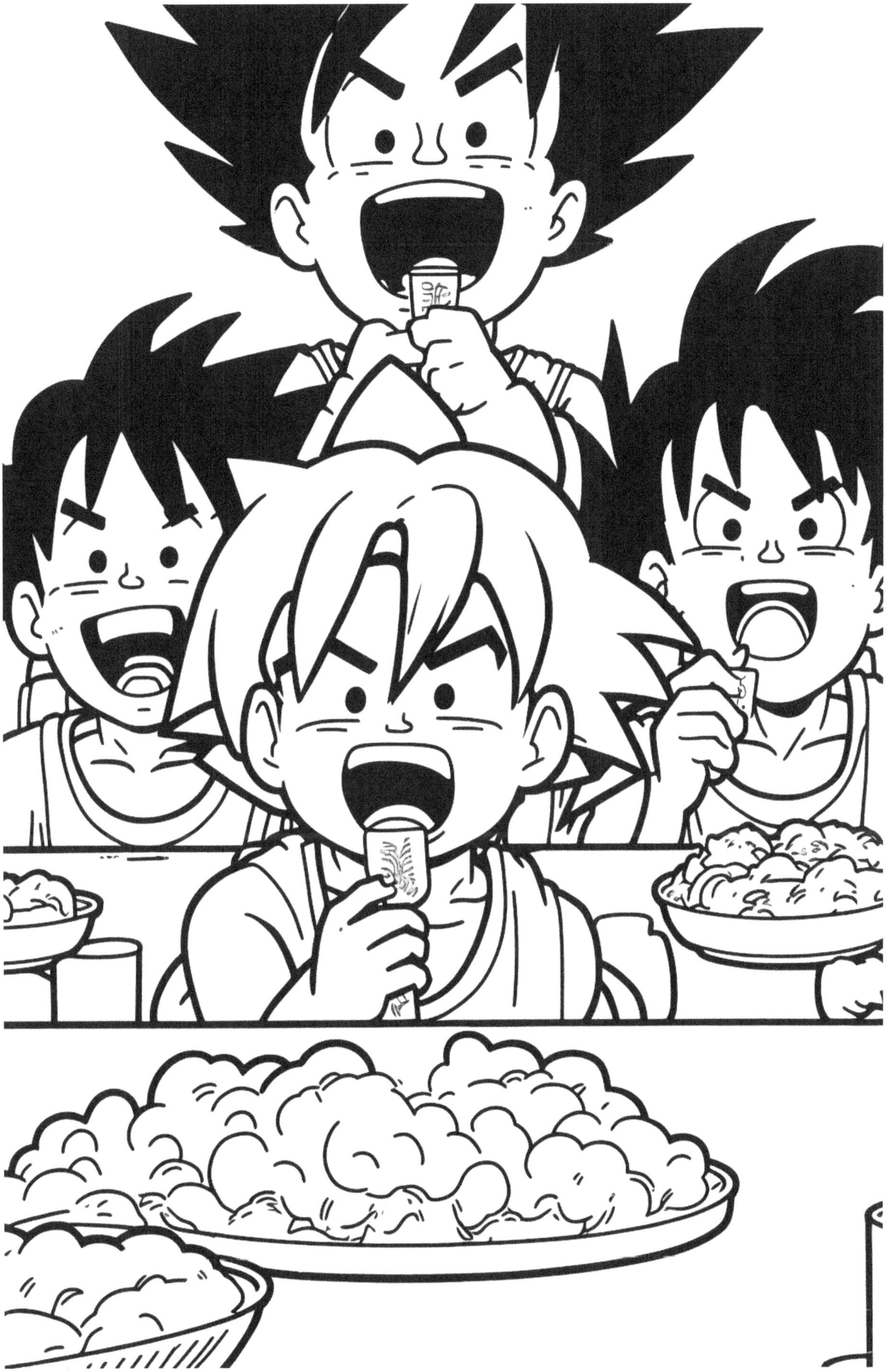

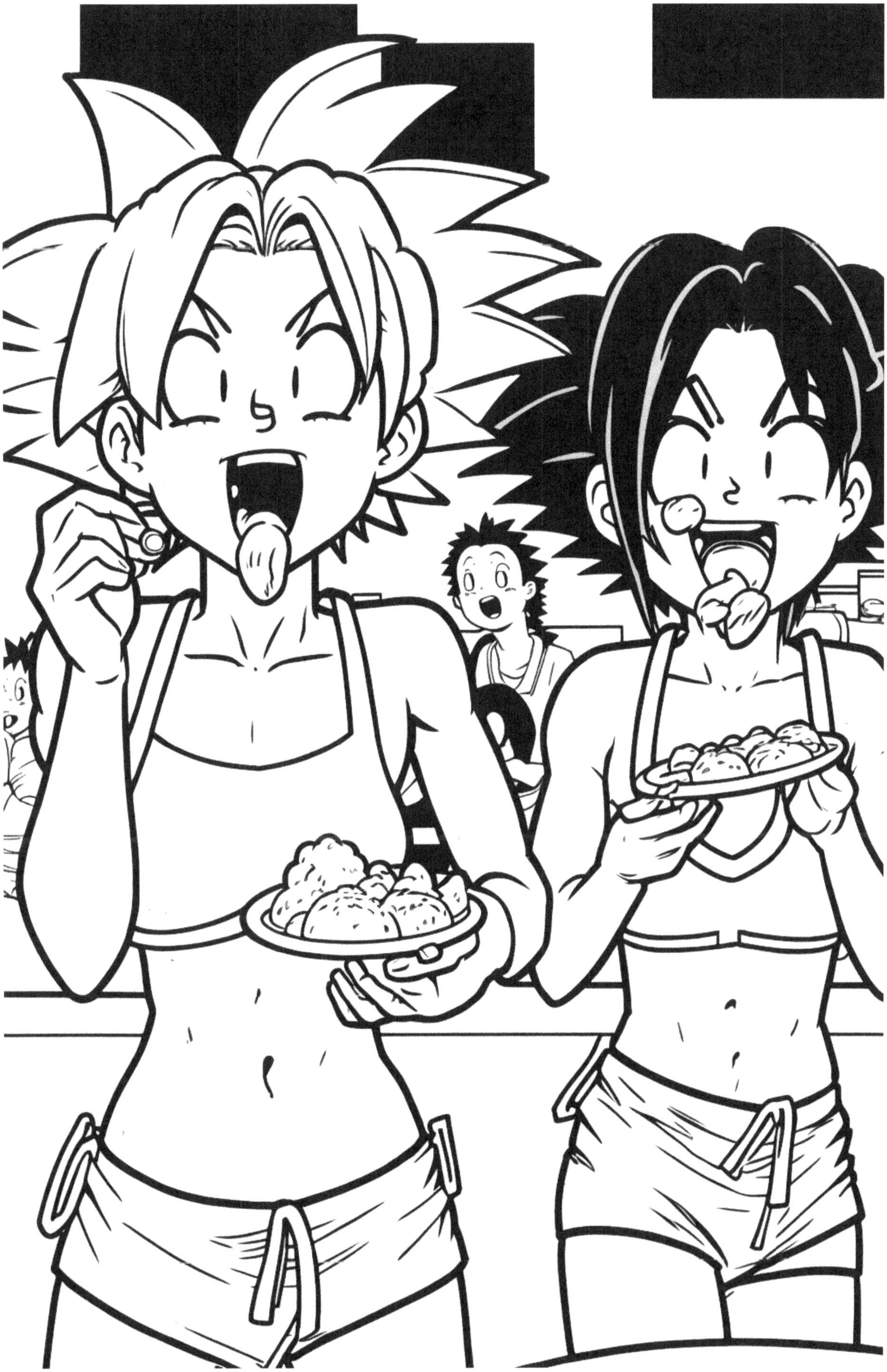

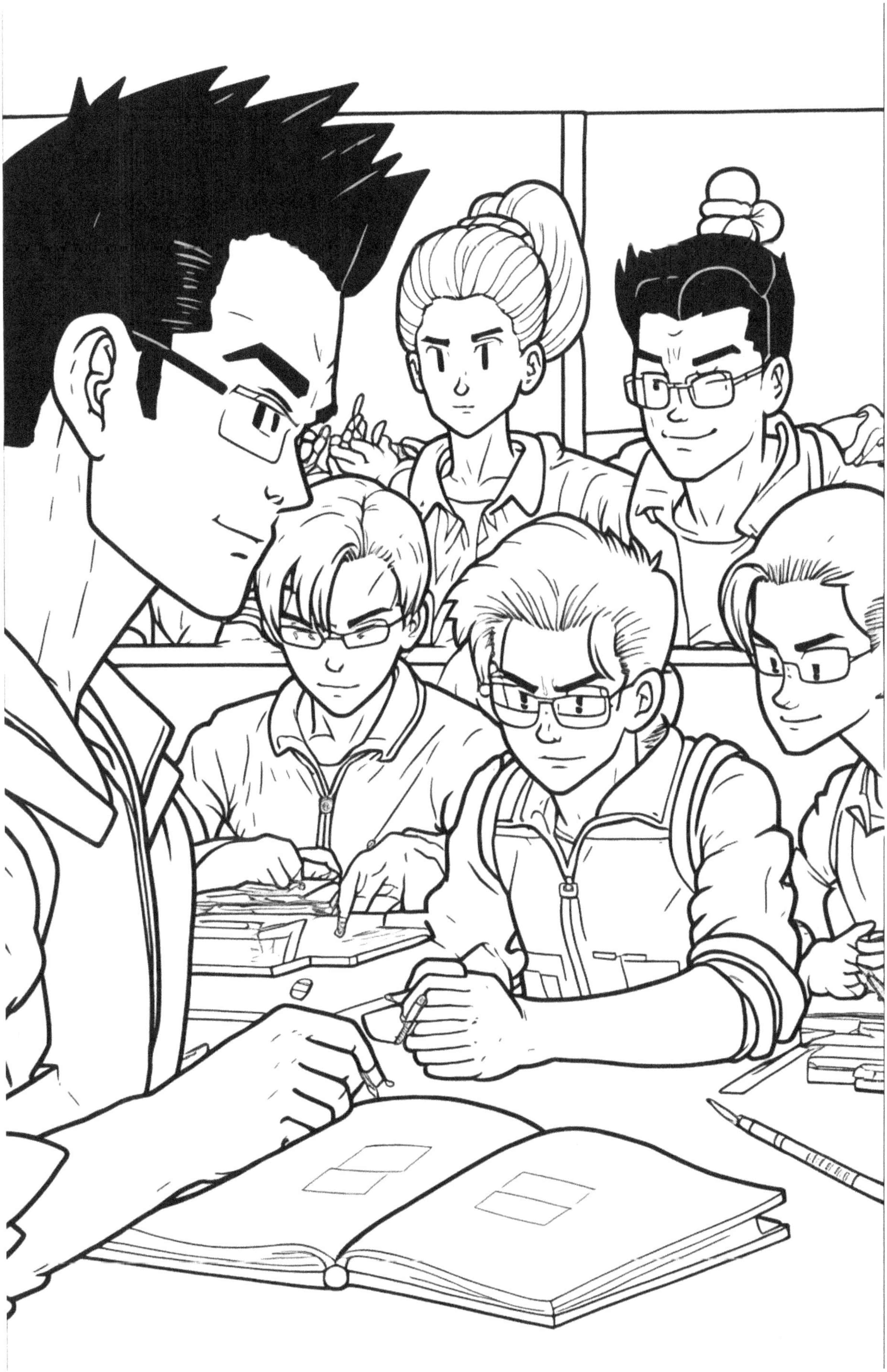

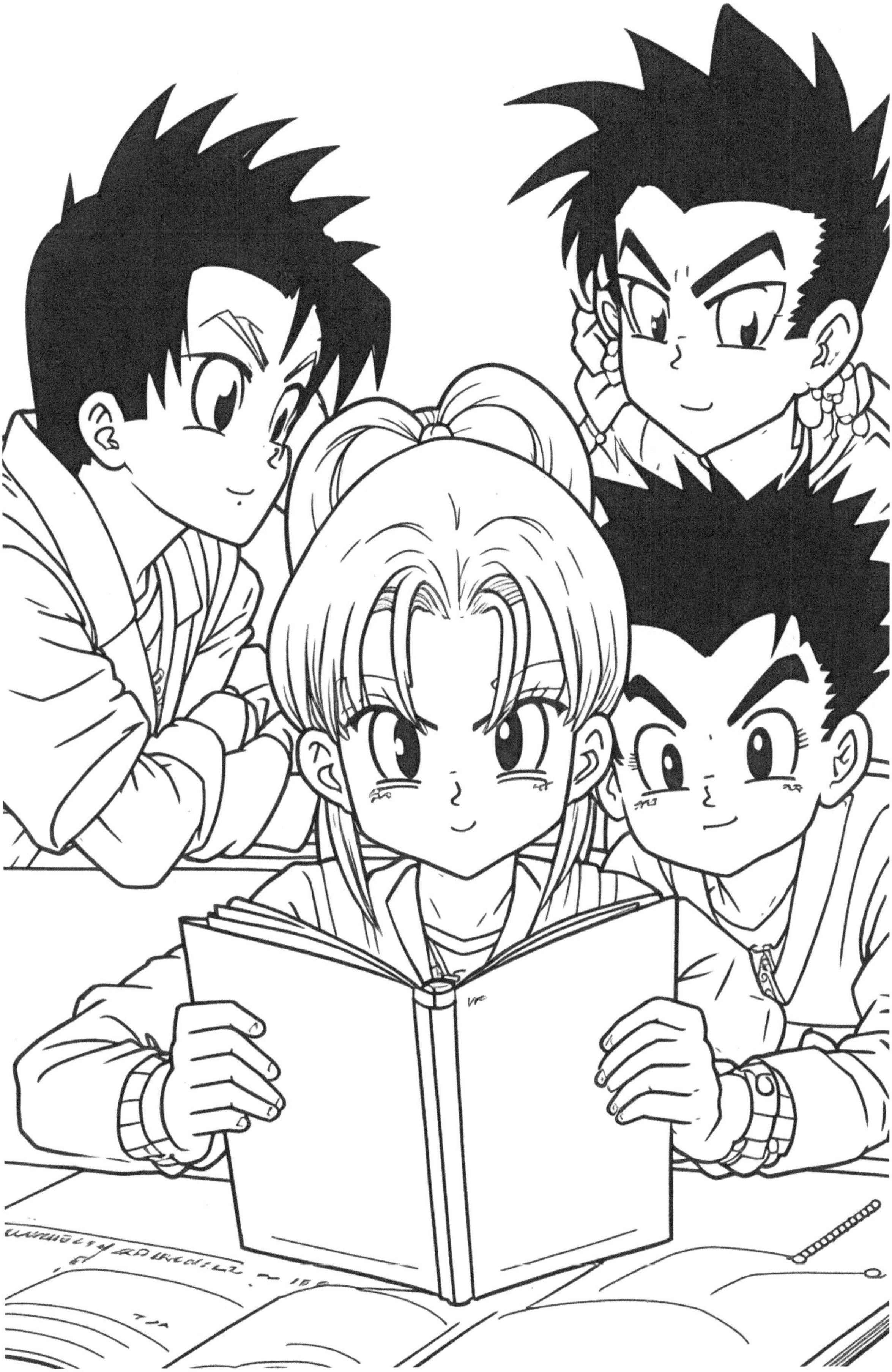

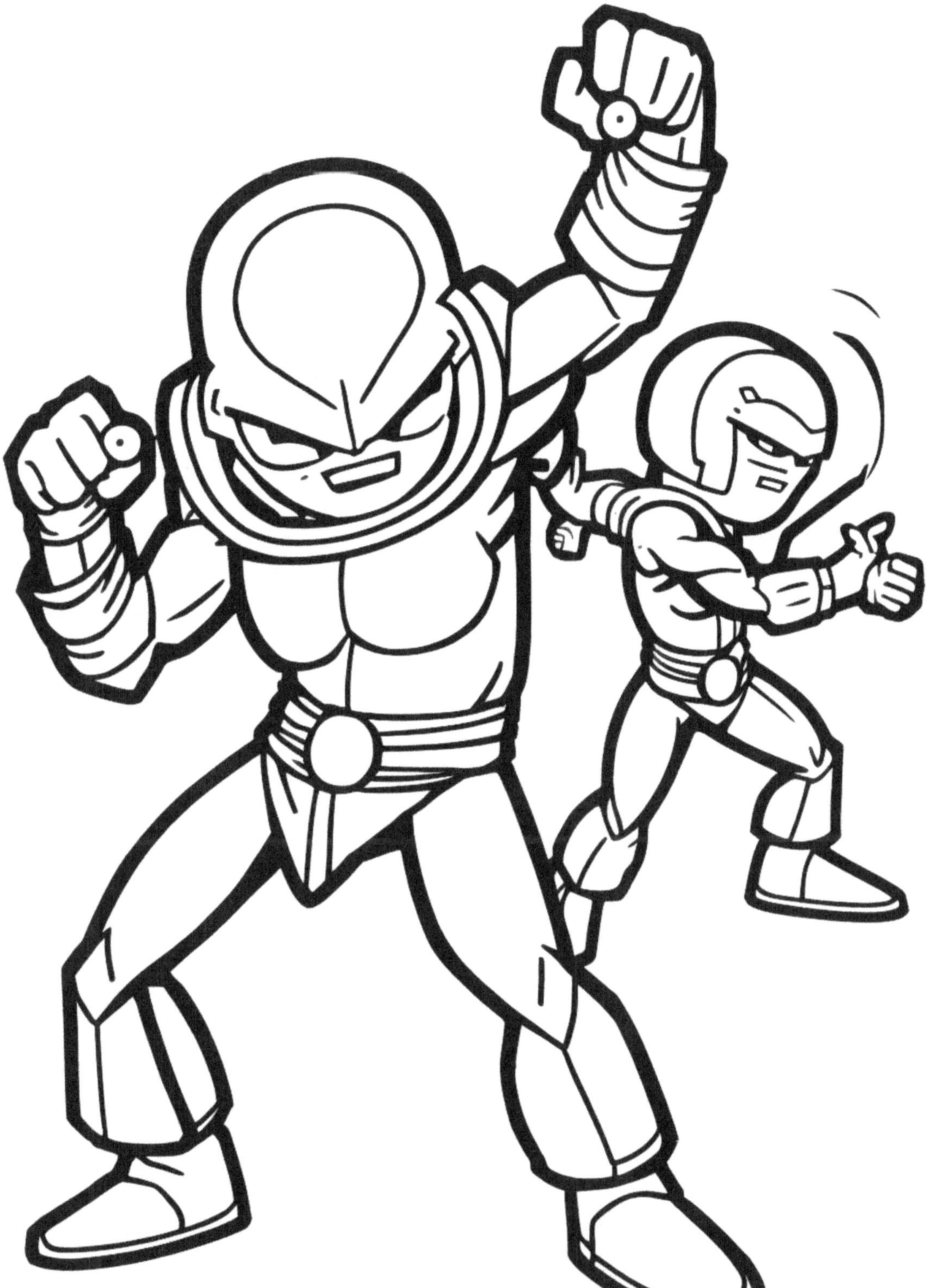

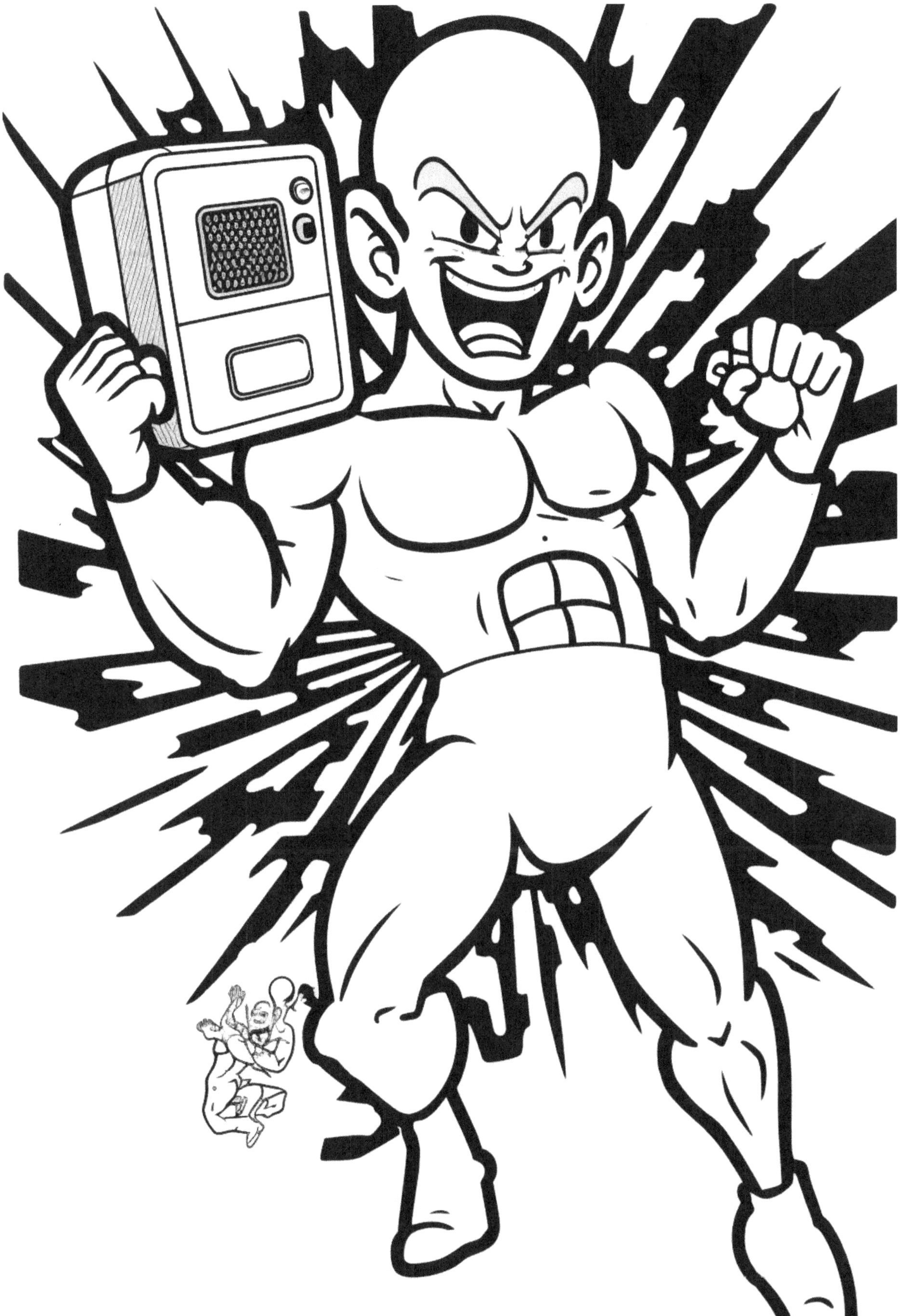

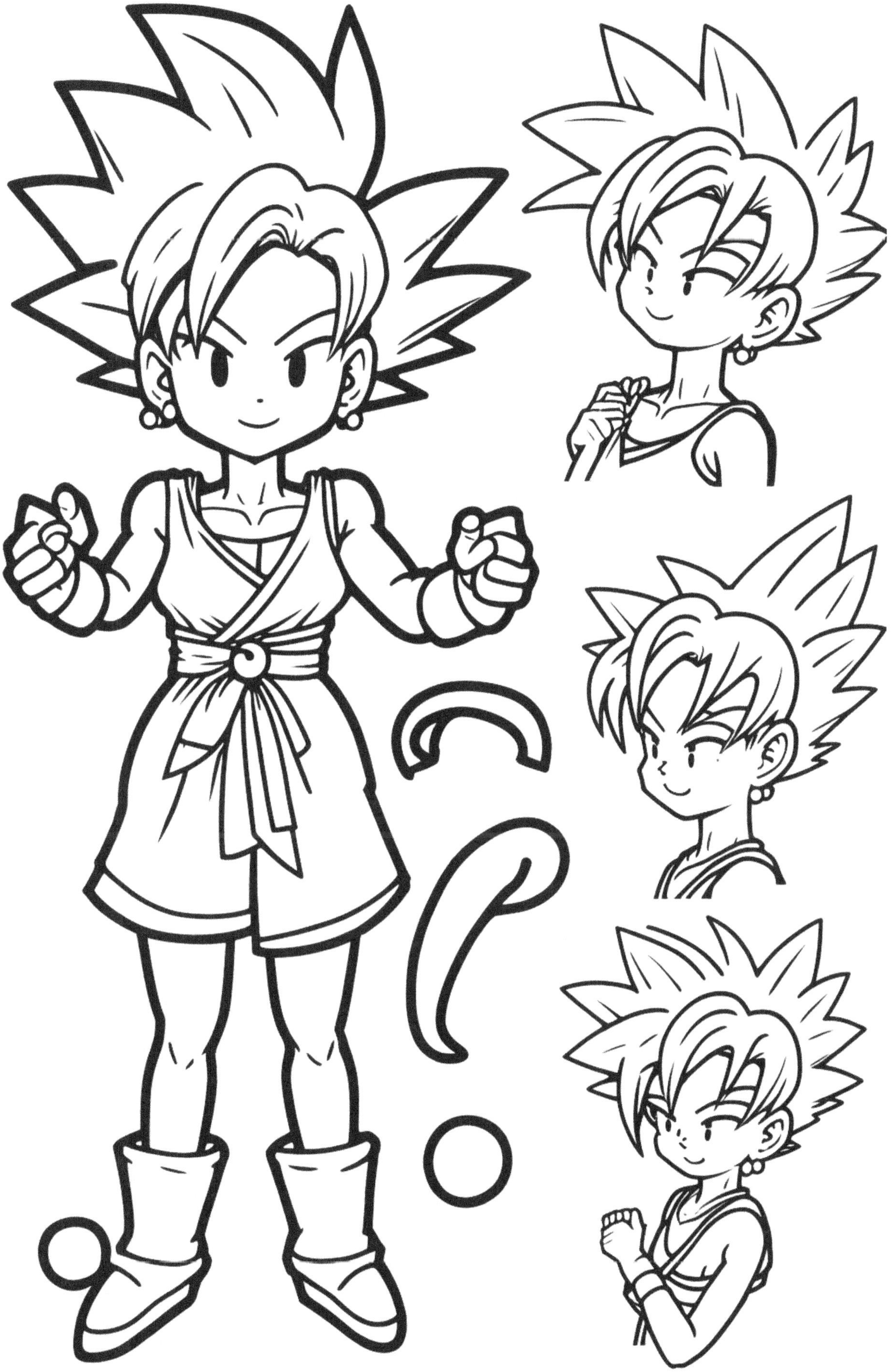

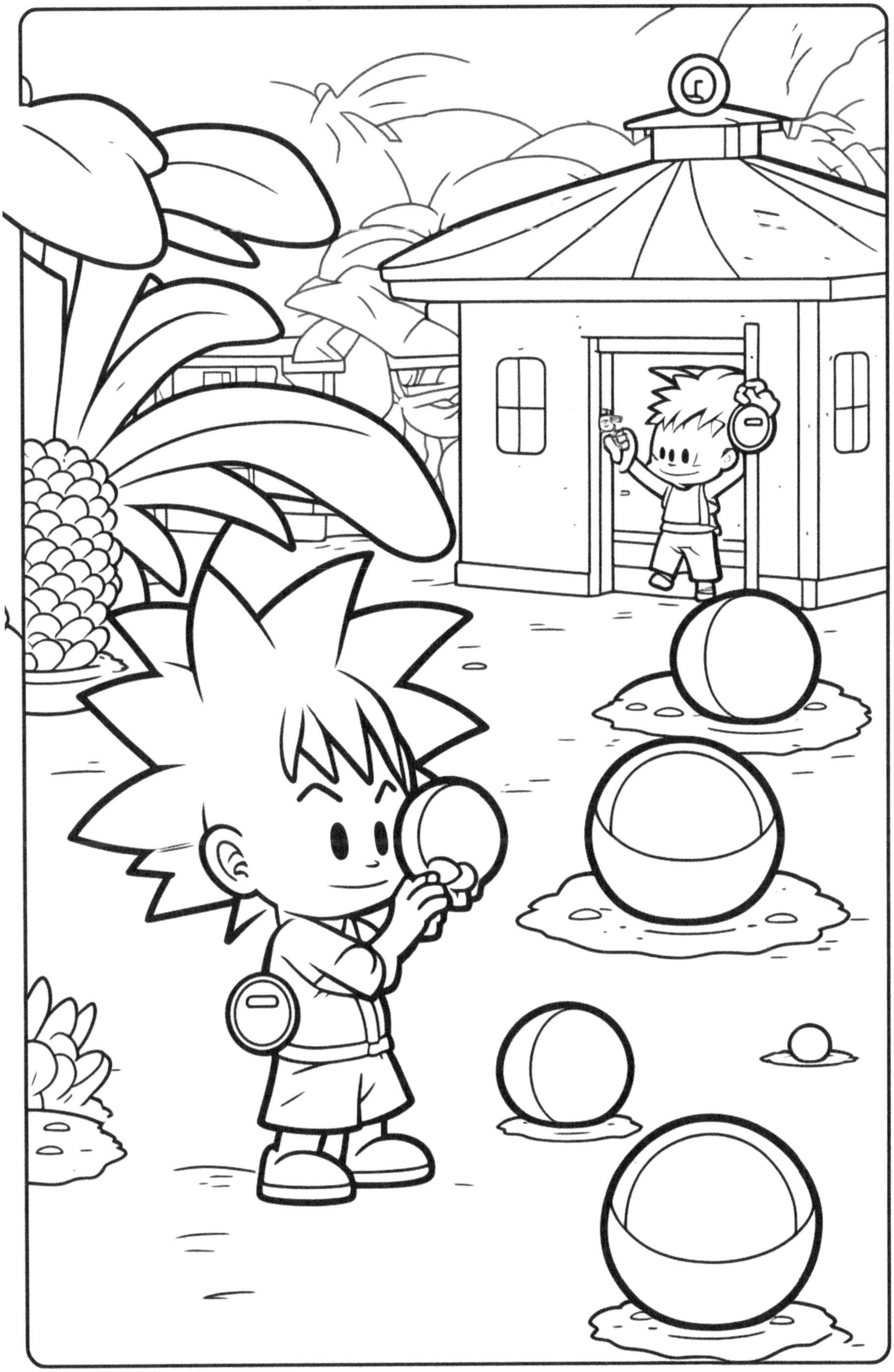

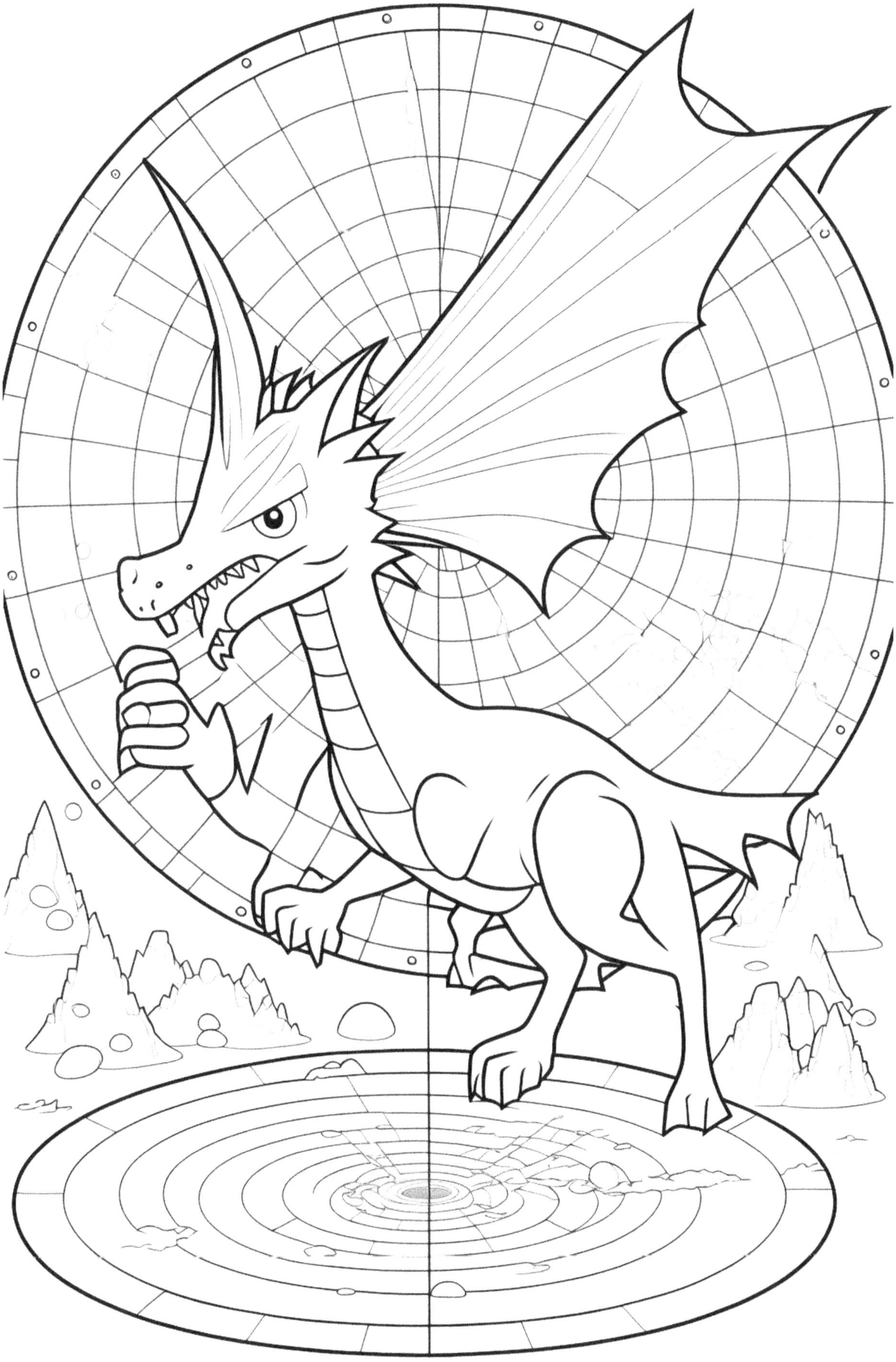

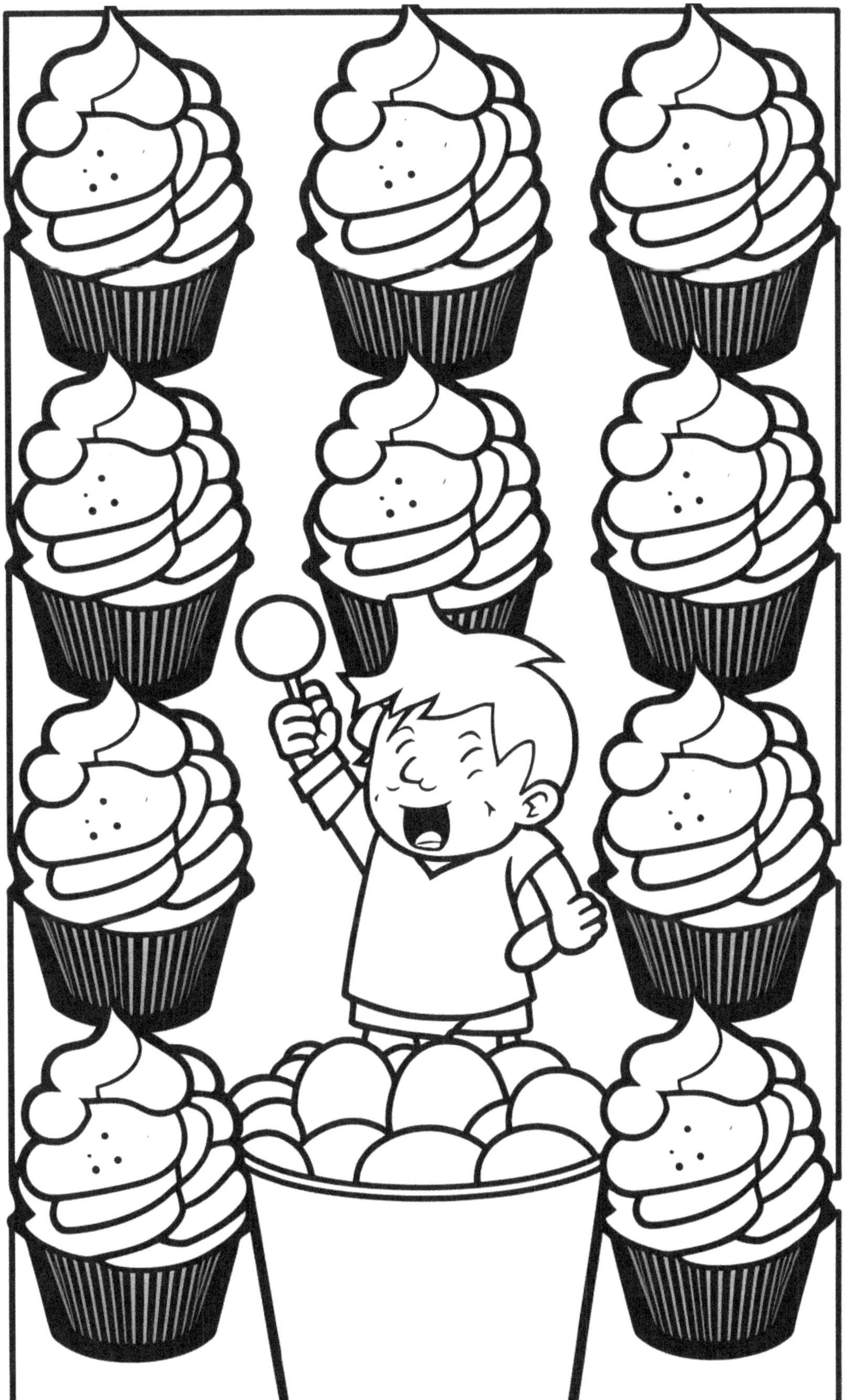

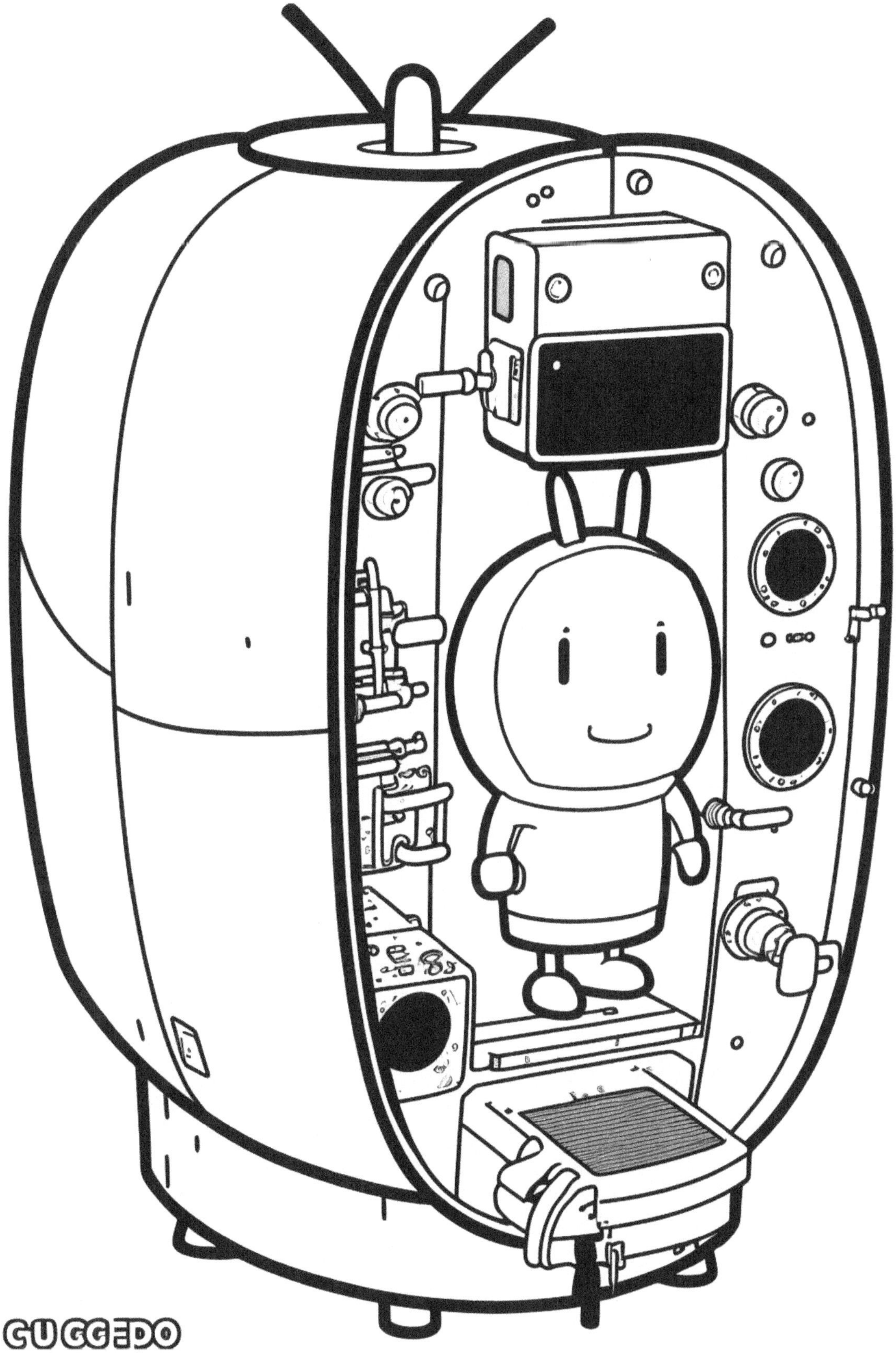

GU GGEDO

SO AGIEMCAS CAMEIBCIMEON/GO ARTGGTSOIN

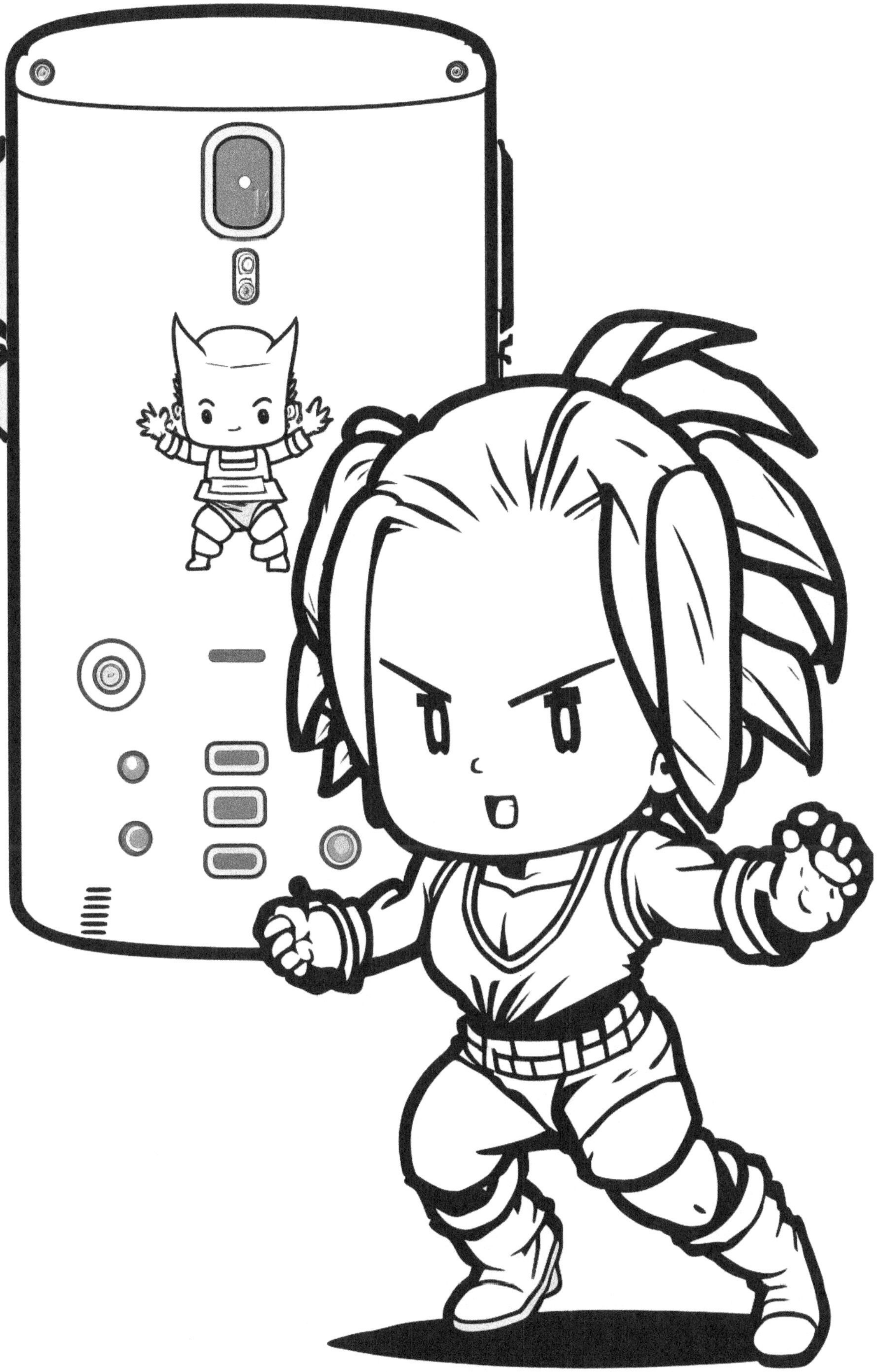

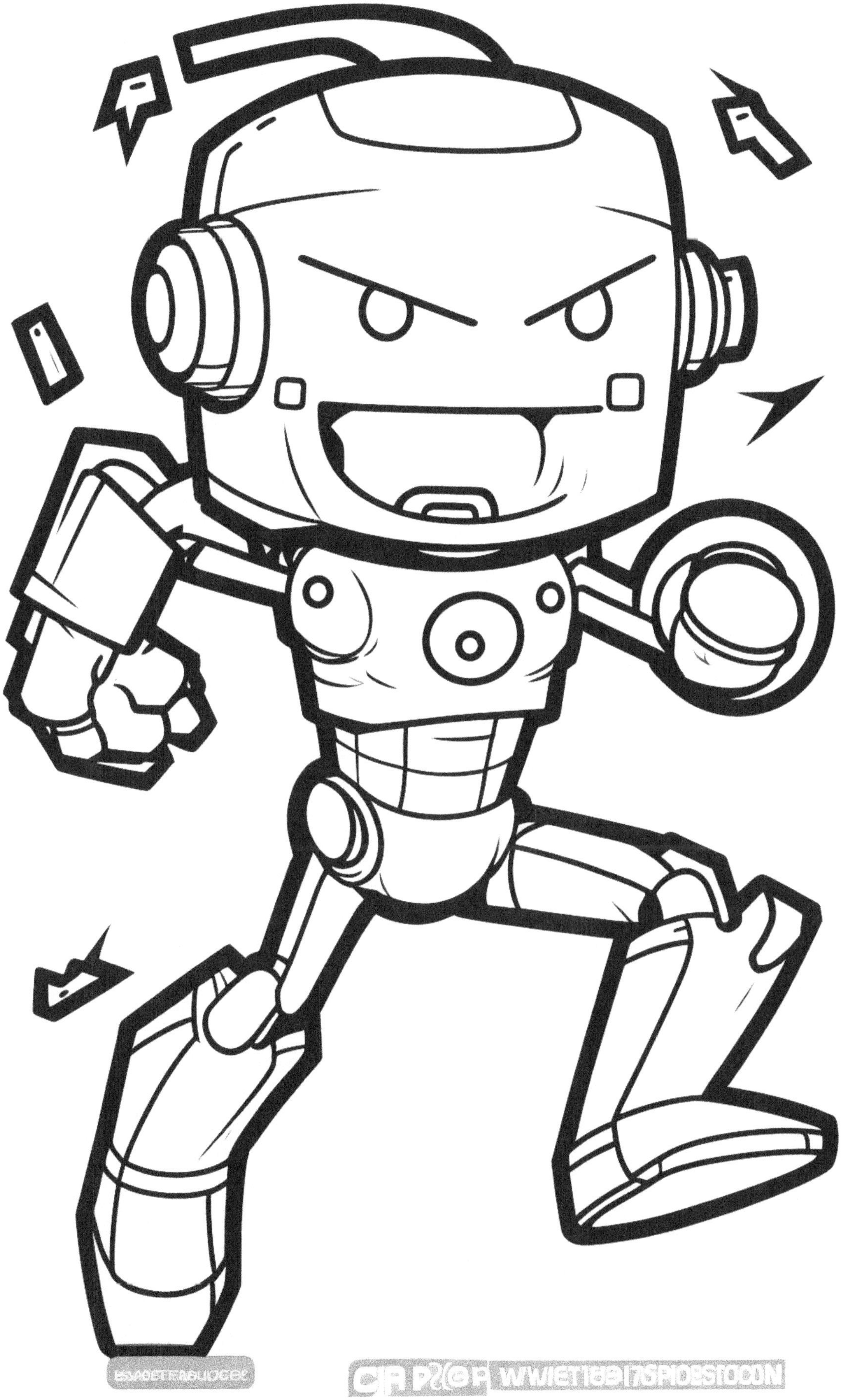

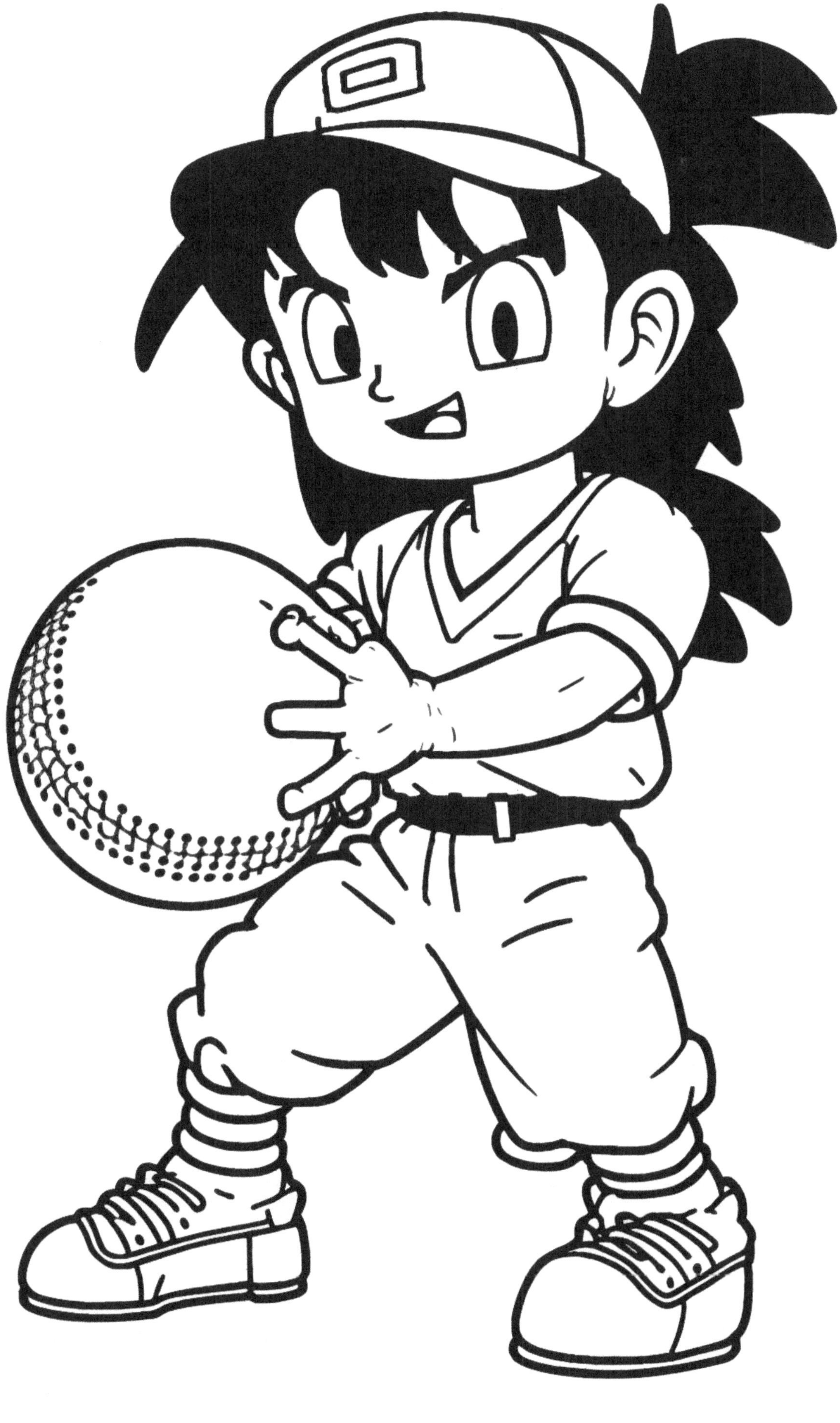

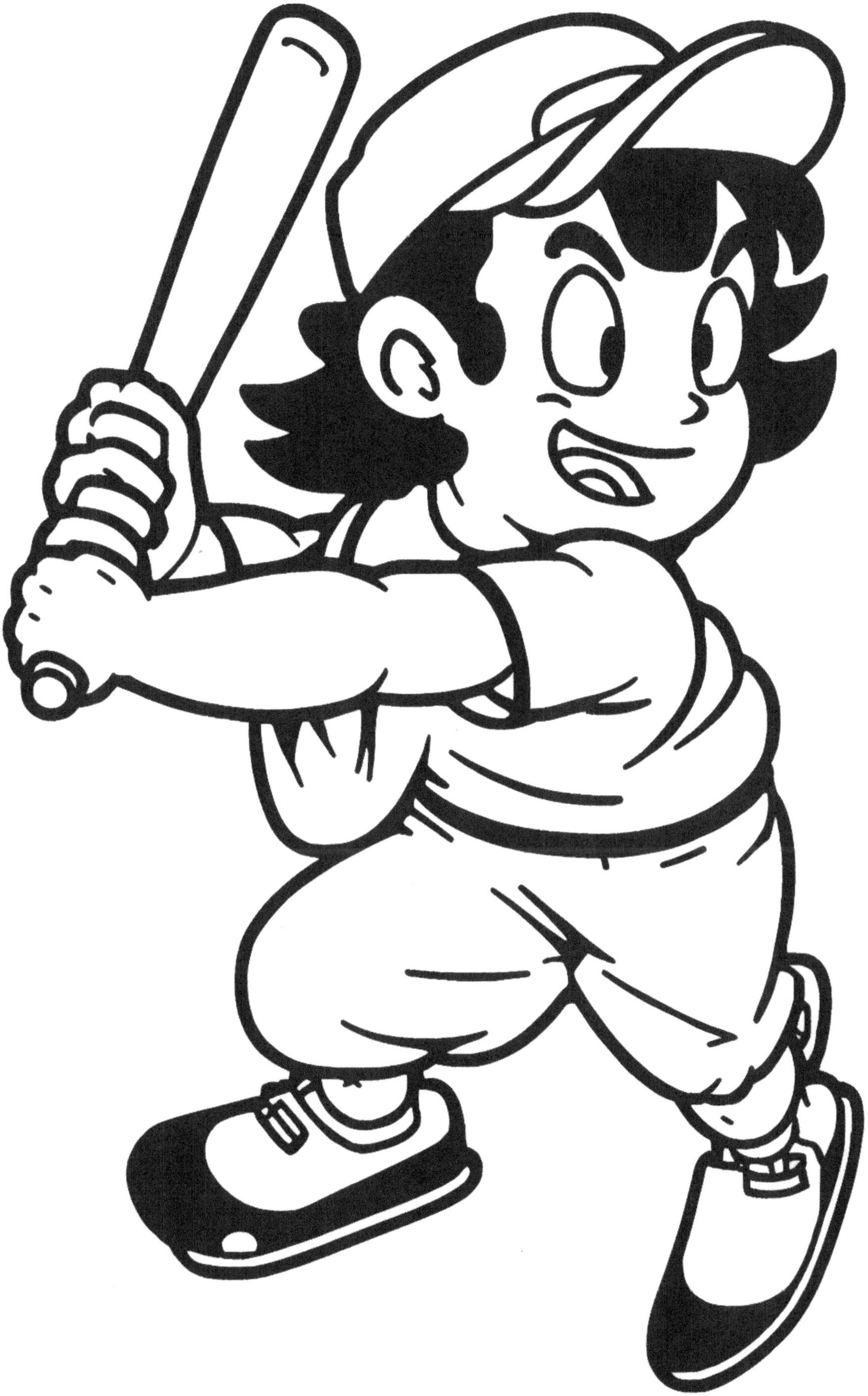

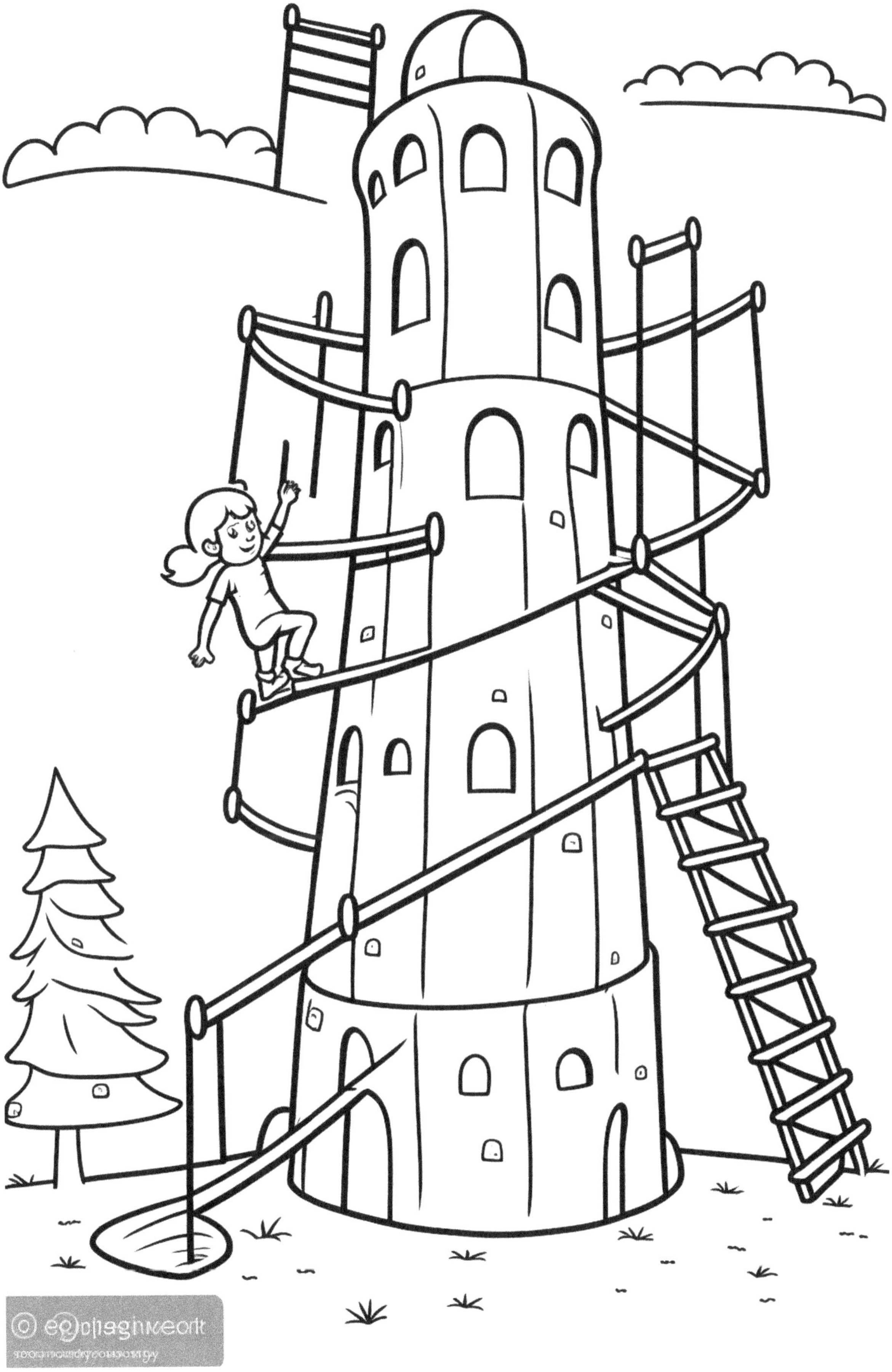

www.ingramcontent.com/pod-product-compliance
Lightning Source LLC
Chambersburg PA
CBHW082228290526
45794CB00009B/3721
* 9 7 9 8 8 7 1 7 7 5 7 3 8 *